ENGLAND'S HERO
A Tribute To David Seaman

ENGLAND'S HERO

A TRIBUTE TO DAVID SEAMAN

Paul Elliott

EDINBURGH AND LONDON

First published in Great Britain in 1997 by
MAINSTREAM PUBLISHING COMPANY (EDINBURGH) LIMITED
7 Albany Street
Edinburgh EH1 3UG

ISBN 1 84018 014 5

A catalogue record for this book is available from the British Library

Designed by Ian McPherson

Printed and bound in Great Britain by The Bath Press Colourbooks, Glasgow

Contents

AUTHOR'S ACKNOWLEDGEMENTS

With thanks to the following publications for invaluable source material: *The Daily Mail, The Sun, The Daily Mirror, The Evening Standard* and *Four Four Two.*

A dedication: For Percy, The Jonah, The Bird Dancer, The Gumby, Pat, Vic, Peace, The Bulky Form, The Voice Of Doom, The Nutter. And for Leo, rest in peace.

National Hero

Football's coming home. It is June, 1996, and these three words are on the lips of everyone in England. The Euro 96 championships have created football hysteria the like of which hasn't been experienced since England hosted and won the World Cup way back in 1966. Now, everywhere you go, people are talking about football; the last England game, the next England game, Alan Shearer's last goal. On June 22, nationwide euphoria reaches fever pitch as England line up to take on Spain in the Euro 96 quarter-finals.

In the previous match, England didn't merely beat Holland, they crushed them, 4–1. So as the English and Spanish teams emerge from the Wembley tunnel on a stiflingly warm summer afternoon, the sell-out 75,000 crowd is in expectant mood. The England fans are ready for another party. 'Three Lions', England's new footie anthem, booms around Wembley. 'It's coming home, it's coming home, it's coming. Football's coming home...'

But after 90 minutes and a nail-biting half an hour of extra time, the game is still goalless. If anything, England are lucky to still be in the competition. Spain have been the better team, and would surely have won were it not for the safe hands – and feet – of England goalkeeper David Seaman.

So now it's time for penalties – and once again, English hopes rest on Seaman's broad shoulders. Seaman's penalty

David's astonishing career always seems to keep coming back to penalty shoot-outs and how to win them

save from Gary McAllister proved the turning point in England's titanic battle with Scotland in the group stage, but can the big man do it again?

Shearer scores England's first spot-kick; Hierro misses for Spain. Then, after each side has scored their next two penalties, Stuart Pearce steps up to take England's fourth. Pearce, of course, missed one of the penalties that led to English defeat in the World Cup semi-final against Germany six years previously. The tension is unbearable, but not for Pearce. The hardman defender blasts the kick home, punches the air, roars at the England fans, then shoots a steely glare at Seaman, imploring him to do it .

The big 'keeper walks to the goal with the crowd chanting his name. Nadal steps up, hits it hard and true, but Seaman is quickly down to his left, turning the ball around the post with a strong hand.

Cue mayhem. Seaman, normally so calm and reserved, dances a jig of delight across the box, clapping his huge hands, his expression a mixture of elation and disbelief. Suddenly he is swamped by team-mates. Nick Barmby is first, grinning like a maniac, then Steve Stone, bouncing up and down deliriously. Then Seaman is grabbed by Tim Flowers, his international understudy. Flowers' beaming face says everything about the team spirit in the England camp. No petty jealousies here: Flowers is just happy that England have won, and is in a hurry to congratulate the hero of the moment.

And the celebrations don't end there. Seaman's face is barely visible as Sol Campbell, then Darren Anderton and then Teddy Sheringham hug him and ruffle that immaculate hair. When David finally emerges from the mob, he seems dazed and unsure what to do. Adrenaline still pumping like mad, he simply raises both arms in a clenched-fist salute to the crowd.

"He is second to none in world football"

As Nadal walks past Seaman to shake hands with the England players, his despair is in total contrast to Seaman's joy. But that, as they say, is football. And David Seaman knows better than most the highs and lows of the game.

On June 22, 1996, David Seaman stood tall as a national hero, the man who had quite literally saved England. He looks back on that day as the proudest of his life.

But it hasn't always been so easy for the lad from the Yorkshire steeltown of Rotherham. David has suffered his fair share of disappointments and heartbreak on his journey from schoolboy Leeds United fan to England's number one. Yet he always believed in his heart that he could be up there with the best, and it is this unshakeable self-belief that has pulled him through the bad times.

Confidence. Determination. Dedication. Focus. Natural ability. And sheer hard graft. These are the qualities which have made David Seaman one of the world's greatest goalkeepers.

He might even be the greatest. It's a subject that has been debated by football fans all over the planet. Of course there are many outstanding 'keepers in world football; Peter Schmeichel of Manchester United and Denmark, Victor Baia of Barcelona and Portugal, Angelo Peruzzi of Juventus and Italy. And David Seaman is the equal of any of them.

When David signs autographs with the nickname Safe Hands, it's a bit of fun, certainly, but it is also a statement of fact.

When England were dumped out of Euro 96 – again by the old enemy Germany, again at the semi-final stage, again on penalties – the departing England coach Terry Venables paid a glowing tribute to David Seaman: "He is second to none in world football," Venables stated. "He is the complete all-rounder as a professional and a person."

The euphoria of Euro 96 might have died down, but the simple truth remained: David Seaman had not only established himself as England's first choice 'keeper; he had also established himself on the world stage as one of international football's greatest talents. Not bad for a lad who, at age 16, was told that he'd never make it in pro football. But again, it all comes back to self-belief.

"Of course I make mistakes," David confessed to *The Sun* newspaper. "But the top goalkeepers, whom with all due modesty I consider myself among, make far fewer mistakes than outfield players. Strikers miss more than we do."

If that sounds like goalkeepers' logic, that's because it is. Everyone in football will tell you that 'keepers are a breed apart. Some will even tell you that the men between the sticks are a few sandwiches short of a picnic. Let's face it, you'd have to be a bit mad to want to stand with your back

David Seaman: The equal of any 'keeper, anywhere

to the Kop for 45 minutes on a freezing January night with only a few thousand sarcastic Liverpool fans for company. But to David Seaman, it's all part of the fun, and after his Euro 96 heroics, he gets treated a little differently whenever Arsenal play away from home.

When the Gunners visited Anfield in the first weeks of the 1996–7 FA Carling Premiership season, the welcome Seaman received from the Liverpool fans took the Arsenal 'keeper's breath away and brought a lump to his throat. As David walked out toward the Kop for the second half, all he could see was a mass of smiling faces and clapping hands. David says the reception from the Kop fans literally stopped him in his tracks. He turned to team-mate Ray Parlour, said something along the lines of 'Bleedin' hell – how about that?', and returned the Scouse fans' applause.

Seaman's mentor, Arsenal goalkeeping coach Bob Wilson, said that David had truly captured the imagination of the English public during Euro 96. That memorable night at Anfield confirmed the man's status as a national hero.

He established himself on the world stage

Seaman's life has been changed by the saves he's made

The Liverpool crowd are as knowledgeable as any in the country. They know when they see quality, and they see plenty of it in David Seaman.

Undoubtedly, Euro 96 changed David Seaman's life. He was the only England player to get a medal out of the competition, collecting the MBE on New Year's Eve 1996. And with this award, Buckingham Palace was simply reaffirming public opinion.

The English people believe that the country's footballing destiny is safe in David Seaman's hands. He's a man you can trust.

George Graham, the former Arsenal manager who bought Seaman in 1990 for a then record fee for a 'keeper, described Seaman as the perfect professional.

"There are some people you know you can trust, and David is one," Graham stated. "He is a great professional and a genuine man."

David himself says that following Euro 96, wherever he goes throughout the country, he is welcomed like an old friend. Of course the Arsenal fans chant his name and shake his hand if they meet him in the street, but now the reaction is the same at every club in the land.

Such universal acclaim has taken the unassuming and laid-back Seaman by surprise, but he is delighted by all the fuss, and says he now realises just how much the success of the national team means to the people of England. He also realises exactly how huge a responsibility rests in his hands.

TV personality, journalist, sports fanatic and fellow Yorkshireman Michael Parkinson reckoned that the enduring image of Euro 96 was one of David Seaman at a party hosted by Sir David Frost. A throng of celebrities from the world of sport and showbiz were all queuing for Seaman's autograph. The man himself stood there signing everything that was pushed under his nose, all the time grinning from ear to ear.

It was the same when David and his girlfriend Debbie attended a premiere of the Madonna movie *Evita* in London's West End in December 1996. As David and Debbie entered the theatre, they walked past a mass of paparazzi photographers, who are regarded as a pretty hard-nosed bunch, but when they spotted England's number one, they all cheered, pointed at David and chanted 'Seamo! Seamo!'.

And there was a similar reaction on the day that David and Debbie went to the Wimbledon tennis championships with Paul Ince and his wife Claire, just a few weeks after Euro 96 had ended. As the foursome settled into their seats to watch four-times champion Pete Sampras playing on Centre Court, the whole crowd stood to cheer. Seaman thought that something spectacular must have happened on court without him noticing – until he realised that everyone was looking at him and Paul Ince! And what made it even more amazing was seeing Pete Sampras leading the applause.

Such attention doesn't bother David Seaman. The big man just laughs it off. As anyone who knows him will testify, David is one of life's gigglers. One journalist even joked that if he were a comedian about to perform an opening night at the London Palladium, he'd send David Seaman free tickets in the front row so he'd be sure of a few laughs. Make that plenty of laughs. As George Graham recalled to *The Sun*: "I always picture David in the middle of the dressing room laughing at the antics of others. If you are a bad joke teller, make David your mate because he will fall about no matter how much you fluff the punchline."

As Seaman himself explains: "If someone tells a joke and it's a crap joke, I can't go, 'That's shit'. I haven't got that

"He is a great pro and a genuine man"

Seaman appreciates the incredible highs he's had – he's also known how low the lows can get

in me. You've just got to laugh to make them feel better." Dependable: that's David Seaman. Whether you're a bad comedian or a top flight football manager, you know you can rely on the big Yorkshireman. And that's what you want above all else from a goal'keeper: reliability.

As Terry Venables told the press, post Euro 96: "It is wrong to talk of penalties or individual saves with David Seaman. You don't get an MBE because you have one good day. He is a magnificent influence on his team-mates, whether it's his calm manner or his performances on the field."

Trust Seaman to play down his MBE and pay tribute instead to his Arsenal and England team-mates. Without them, he insisted, he would have accomplished nothing.

"Football is, of course, a team sport," David said after visiting Buckingham Palace. "I dedicate this award to my team-mates."

Few footballers are as self-effacing as David Seaman, but when everybody else is heaping praise on him, proclaiming him the best 'keeper in the world, David himself doesn't need to say anything.

David also knows better than anyone how quickly the fortunes of a goal'keeper can change. After all, it wasn't all that long ago that young David Seaman was a tallish teenage lad playing for a Yorkshire school team and dreaming about getting to the top. It seemed like an awful long way to climb.

And he can still recall walking home in tears after letting in 26 goals in one match. Yes, even David Seaman had to start somewhere.

Nothing Else Matters

David Andrew Seaman was born in Rotherham, Yorkshire on September 19, 1963. Rotherham, like neighbouring Sheffield, is a steel town, but even at an early age, David knew that a job in the steel industry was not for him. He also didn't put too much effort into his school work. Football was what mattered to the young David Seaman. Nothing else.

"I weren't a rebel or anything," David told *The Sunday Times*. "I was just a little bit lazy. And I sacrificed my school work for football."

Knowing this was the case, David's teachers decided to hit the boy where it hurt if he stepped out of line at school. If he got into trouble, Seaman was not given extra homework – he was excluded from physical education lessons. For David this was the worst possible punishment, but both he and his teachers knew that the threat of no PE was the only way they could get him to pay attention in class.

David describes his childhood as a happy one. He kept out of trouble, which isn't the easiest thing to do when you tower over just about every other kid at your school. And he played football. A lot of football.

"I was like any other kid who wanted to be a top 'keeper," he recalled. "I loved making the flashy, full-length saves. I still love them, but now I know I must be solid in my all-round game, knowing when I should dive and when I should anticipate."

Big Dave once conceded 26 goals in a school game – there's hope for all of us!

David was advised by his headmaster to take up cricket. The head was well connected to Yorkshire Cricket Club. David admits he was tempted, but football was his first obsession.

David played in goal for various school teams, and remembers his first game for Ferham Road Primary School more vividly than any other. That was the day he conceded 26 goals, and went home in floods of tears.

But it didn't break him. Even at a tender age, David Seaman had guts. One bad day, even one as bad as that, wasn't going to ruin this schoolboy's dream of playing pro football.

And as a Yorkshire lad, there was only one team David wanted to play for – Leeds United. During the late Seventies, David was a regular on the terraces at Elland Road. At that time, most Leeds supporters idolised the long-haired midfield genius Tony Currie, but not David Seaman. His hero was the stalwart Leeds 'keeper David Harvey.

For years, Seaman dreamed of following in Harvey's footsteps, of wearing the green jersey for Leeds United, so imagine the boy's excitement when United took him on to their books as an apprentice in 1979. David left school at the age of 16 without taking a single exam. His last day at school was on a Friday. The following Monday he was nervously starting out at Leeds.

But the dream turned sour. Three years into his apprenticeship, David was told by the Leeds boss Eddie Gray that he had no future in football.

Ironically, the goalkeeper who turned professional at Leeds that season was John Lukic. Lukic would later be replaced by Seaman at Arsenal, and would follow a second spell at Leeds with a second spell at Arsenal as number two to Seaman.

Lukic recalls being "gobsmacked" when Leeds dispensed with the young Seaman. Now, says Lukic, David Seaman is acknowledged as the best, and how Leeds United must rue the day they let him go.

When Eddie Gray showed him the door, David was of course heartbroken. Even now, he considers this rejection to be one of the biggest disappointments of his career. For the 19-year-old Seaman, who had built his whole life around football, it seemed like the end of the world. And of course, it hurt even more that the club who had released him were the club he had supported for as long as he could remember.

Leeds had told him he wasn't good enough to be a professional footballer, so what now? David considered a new career. He thought about taking a job as a baker's delivery boy. There were a lot of tears and many long nights of soul-searching.

And then came a day when David's dad put his arm round his dejected son and told him to pick himself up and get on with playing football. That, says David, is how Yorkshire folk deal with their problems. They stand up straight and get on with it.

Fortunately, a new opportunity was not too long in coming. Martin Wilkinson had been assistant manager at Leeds during Seaman's apprenticeship and had been impressed by the young 'keeper. By 1982 Wilkinson had moved to Peterborough United and he offered Seaman a trial. Seaman passed the test. "I didn't even know where Peterborough was," Seaman recalls, "but anything was better than being thrown out of the game."

Seaman celebrates: His hero was Bruce Grobbelaar, a clowning 'keeper who entertained the crowds

Seaman spent three seasons at London Road, making a total of 91 first team appearances for Peterborough before he was spotted by Birmingham City manager Ron Saunders.

When Birmingham signed him, David's confidence grew and grew. Ron Saunders was a well-respected figure in British football who had won the European Cup with Birmingham's arch rivals Aston Villa. If Ron Saunders thought David Seaman was good enough, that was all the encouragement that Seaman needed. The pain of rejection by Leeds was fading fast.

In two seasons at St Andrews, David played 75 first team games, but when the Blues were relegated to the former Division Two at the end of the 1985–6 season, he felt it was time to move on.

"The top division was the only place to be," David told *The Sun*, "and when they were relegated I had to think about my future."

David's performances at Birmingham had alerted Jim Smith at Queens Park Rangers, and the ever-shrewd 'Bald Eagle' was quick to snap up the 23-year-old David Seaman for a bargain £220,000

Smith said that when he bought Seaman, Birmingham told him that the 'keeper had the potential to play for England. Smith didn't doubt it when he saw Seaman perform.

In Seaman's second season at QPR, with an England call-up beckoning, Smith told the London *Evening Standard*: "He's big and strong and makes things look easy. And he doesn't get uptight under pressure. He's very calm. He's a nice, quiet lad – perhaps even a bit too quiet on the field."

Even then, Seaman's reputation for unflappability was well established. Surprising, then, to hear him citing Bruce Grobbelaar as his favourite contemporary. Grobbelaar's eccentric – some would say madcap – approach to the art of goalkeeping is the polar opposite of David Seaman's coolness, but Seaman is full of admiration for the colourful Zimbabwean international.

"I didn't know where Peterborough was!"

"I think the game is about entertainment and I like the flamboyance of Bruce Grobbelaar," Seaman told *The Sun*.

That said, Seaman has built his own reputation on solidity. He is not known as Mr Reliable for nothing. And it is his consistency which so impressed Arsenal manager George Graham.

Graham modelled his Arsenal teams in the oldest traditions of the club. Strong defence was the rock on which Arsenal's 1988–9 championship success was built. And when the Gunners failed to retain the title in the following season, Graham looked to improve his squad, starting, inevitably, with the defence and goalkeeper.

Seaman's massive frame makes him difficult to see past, let alone beat...

A thoughtful moment in training with Arsenal

Well, you can't stop 'em all...

Graham's admiration for David Seaman was well-known. For months on end, press stories had linked Seaman with a move across the capital, but Graham was forced to wait almost two years to get his man, during which time there was talk of Seaman signing for Arsenal's great rivals Tottenham Hotspur! In 1988, Spurs boss Terry Venables tried to lure Seaman to White Hart Lane, but Seaman stayed put. Venables bought Norwegian international Erik Thorstvedt instead. Arsenal fans were happy with John Lukic, who had, after all, helped the Gunners win the Championship in '89, but George Graham knew better. When Arsenal and QPR met during the 1989–90 season, Arsenal fans taunted Seaman with chants of "You'll never play for Arsenal". Seaman merely shrugged, smiled and took it on the chin. The Arsenal fans were showing their loyalty to John Lukic, rather than any animosity towards Seaman, but it was David Seaman who wore the number one shirt for the Gunners when the 1990–1 season began with a friendly tournament at Wembley in August. For David Seaman, the big time had finally arrived.

Seaman works incredibly hard on improving his game with his coach, ex-Arsenal 'keeper Bob Wilson

GOTCHA! DAVID SEAMAN ON THE SECRET OF SAVING PENALTIES

"Bob Wilson has always suggested standing still and then going for the ball when the kick is made, in the belief that some kicks will go straighter than intended and well-struck ones into the corner are impossible to save. I disagree. I decide which way to go by looking at the opponent's run-up."

"The pressure on these occasions isn't on the goalkeeper, it's on the taker. You can dive one way, it hits you, and you're a hero."

"I always fancy my chances at spotkicks, and I have a pretty good record, most memorably when I helped Arsenal win that Cup Winners' Cup semi-final penalty shoot-out against Sampdoria. In the Scotland game in Euro 96 I was determined to stand big for as long as was possible in the hope of psyching out McAllister. As he ran up I could tell by the way he was shaping that it would go to my right. And even though the ball came back off my elbow, it was not a case of luck. I'd set my body right for the block, and top goalkeepers know that you have to use all parts of your body."

"My performance in our win over Scotland in Euro 96 was without doubt the best of my career, given the context of the game and the circumstances when I made my contributions. When the final whistle blew my initial reaction was one of sheer relief."

"I really loved the penalty shoot-outs. That is the only time a goalkeeper gets the chance to grab all of the headlines."

Seaman's strength of character has enabled him to overcome the setbacks – like Nayim's lob in the Cup Winners' Cup Final

Running out for Arsenal: Seaman is a hero with the Highbury faithful

Champion!

"If you pay for the best, you get the best." So said Arsenal manager George Graham when he signed David Seaman for £1.3m in May 1990. The fee was a record for a British goalkeeper. Seaman insisted that the size of the fee was not a burden. In fact, he was proud to be recognised as Britain's most expensive 'keeper. And once the Seaman deal went through, George Graham immediately recouped £1m by selling former first-choice keeper John Lukic to Leeds, the club where both he and Seaman had begun their careers.

"David took a lot of stick when I first bought him," Graham added, "because he was replacing John Lukic, who was a fans' favourite. But he won them over."

Seaman himself was also acutely aware of his predecessor's popularity among the Highbury fans, who had sung "There's only one Johnny Lukic" to Seaman when the press leaked news of Graham's intention to sign him as Lukic's replacement.

Seaman says he knew he was taking a risk in replacing such a popular figure and such a reliable performer, but as ever, he had confidence in his own abilities and was desperate to prove that he was good enough to play for one of the very biggest football clubs in Britain.

He was also keen to develop his England career, and felt that a move to Arsenal could only help his international ambitions. Having broken into the England under-21 squad

Seaman doesn't shout at his defence a lot – he just gets on with the job and trusts them to do theirs

while still at Birmingham, Seaman made his full England debut in 1988 in a friendly against Saudi Arabia. At QPR, however, Seaman was receiving limited TV exposure, whereas a club like Arsenal were on the telly week in week out. David wanted more than the handful of caps he had picked up while at Loftus Road. When George Graham came in for him, he didn't need time to think things over.

"I moved to Arsenal from QPR not only to play for a big club but also to experience the extra pressure of performing in big games week in week out," David stated at the start of the 1990–1 season.

He would not be disappointed. There would be many big games that season as Arsenal powered their way to a second league championship title in just three seasons. Right from the opening league fixture – a tricky away match at Wimbledon's 'intimate' old Plough Lane ground – David Seaman was in impeccable form. Arsenal won 3–0

"I wanted a big club"

that day. Seaman caught every cross and made a couple of point-blank saves, and suddenly John Lukic wasn't missed. There were, however, tougher tests to come.

Manchester United visited Highbury on November 28 for a League Cup tie, and put six goals past David Seaman. This

Seaman had to win over the Highbury fans after he replaced the popular John Lukic

David Seaman's remarkable placid temperament has enabled him to overcome many of the bad times

was as many goals as the Gunners had conceded in the previous 14 league games. It was, as they say, just one of those nights. The important thing was how Seaman and Arsenal reacted to this crushing defeat. They answered their critics a few days later with a 3–0 drubbing of league leaders Liverpool at Highbury, Seaman again looking unbeatable.

Another crunch league game came on January 12, 1991, at White Hart Lane against Tottenham. It was a typical North London derby, tight and fiercely competitive, and just like September's corresponding fixture at Highbury, the match finished goalless. This was thanks in no small part to the heroics of Seaman, who denied Spurs' England striker Gary Lineker three times when it seemed certain he would score. After the third of these saves, a fingertip reflex stop from a crisp Lineker snapshot, Seaman turned to the travelling Arsenal fans massed behind his goal and gave them a pumped-up double-fisted victory salute. The fans chanted his name over and over again. David Seaman was now an Arsenal hero.

After that game, Spurs boss Terry Venables, the man who had tried to sign Seaman two years previously, acknowledged the Arsenal 'keeper's "exceptional ability".

Said Seaman: "The game at Spurs was a big one for Arsenal and it produced probably my best ever performance."

Seaman dives at the feet of West Ham's Iain Dowie

Seaman's first season at Highbury was to prove an amazing one...

Relaxed and easy-going off the pitch, Big Dave works hard on his concentration on it...

But there was even better to come. On March 3, Arsenal went to Anfield to play Liverpool in what many observers saw as the championship decider. The teams were neck-and-neck in the title race, but whoever won this game would gain a huge psychological advantage.

Earlier that week, Liverpool had lost manager Kenny Dalglish, who quit the club because the pressure of the job had become too much for him and his family. Yet it was the home side who started the game strongly, attacking fluidly and scaring the pants off the Arsenal fans. But fortunately, not off Seaman. The Gunners' 'keeper pulled off several crucial saves in a first half dominated by Liverpool. Twice Seaman denied John Barnes, first by dropping quickly to his left and tipping a low shot around a post, and later by plucking one of Barnes' trademark chipped free-kicks from the air as it headed for the top corner. When Arsenal scored in the second half through Paul Merson, the Gunners fans knew the points were in the bag.

Nothing was going to get past David Seaman that day. Seaman called it the biggest game of his career thus far.

"It's matches like that I came to Arsenal for," he said, "and it's thrilling to prove to myself that I can excel at that level."

Arsenal won the championship that season in awesome fashion. They lost just one of their 38 league games, conceding just 18 goals. David Seaman kept 24 clean sheets. Only Ray Clemence of Liverpool has conceded fewer goals in an English league season.

George Graham said of Seaman: "I can count his mistakes on the fingers of one hand. He has a truly commanding presence." Seaman also displayed supreme calm even in the most heated of atmospheres. When Arsenal travelled to

David Seaman and Arsenal waited only two years for revenge over Spurs at Wembley...

Old Trafford to play Manchester United on October 20, 1990, just a few weeks before the 6–2 massacre, the tension in the match spilled over to create one of the most controversial incidents ever seen on a British football pitch. Great rivalry had always existed between United and Arsenal, two of the country's biggest and proudest clubs. In addition, a more personal feud had developed between Brian McClair of United and Nigel Winterburn of Arsenal after the Gunners left-back taunted McClair when he missed a late penalty in a cup tie at Highbury. When the pair clashed again at Old Trafford, they sparked a mass brawl. Every player on the pitch was involved. Every player, that is, except David Seaman. Of course, Seaman was further away from the fighting than anyone else, but could anyone really envisage the Arsenal 'keeper getting involved in a scrap? In fact, Seaman appeared bemused by the whole incident. The brawl was eventually broken up and Arsenal went on to win the game 1–0 thanks to more stout defending and more calm goalkeeping from Seaman as the United fans roared their team on, incensed by the violence on the pitch. As a punishment for their unsporting conduct, Arsenal were later docked two points by the Football Association, and United one.

However, even the shock of having two points deducted – an unprecedented action by English football's governing body – was nothing compared to the shock in store for Arsenal on April 14, 1991. This proved to be a black day for all Arsenal fans and especially for David Seaman.

The Gunners faced Spurs again, this time in the FA Cup semi-final. The tie was played at Wembley because demand for tickets was so great, and because both teams were from London. Arsenal were on the verge of repeating their league and Cup double of 1971, but Spurs were determined to put one over their bitter rivals. The pressure

Kicking has become an increasingly important part of the game: and one that David has worked hard on

Seaman prepares to launch another England attack. He made his debut against the mighty Saudi Arabia!

Seaman conceded only 18 goals in the 1990–1 league season, a fantastic achievement

on them was even greater. The club was facing financial disaster, and was on the verge of selling Paul Gascoigne to stay afloat. An FA Cup win and the finance it would bring into the club would keep them alive. Anything less could prove disastrous. Gazza and Spurs ripped into Arsenal like men possessed. 40,000 Arsenal fans looked on in horror as the Gunners went two-nil down inside the opening six minutes of the game.

Paul Gascoigne scored the first with a free-kick from fully 35 yards. It was one of the greatest goals ever scored at Wembley, a vicious strike curled into the top left-hand corner of Seaman's goal.

"It went 'whoosh!' and that was that," Seaman told *The Sun*. "I half-tripped, got a hand to it, but it wasn't quite enough." No 'keeper likes to be beaten from outside the box, especially in a Cup semi-final against the old enemy, but Seaman was more upset by Tottenham's third goal, which clinched the game. Arsenal had pulled themselves back into the match with a goal just before half-time from Alan Smith, but as the Gunners pressed for an equaliser, Gary Lineker broke free to send a shot through Seaman's hands for 3–1. Seaman knows that a goalkeeper of his stature should have saved it. He says now that the defeat left him feeling annoyed rather than devastated, but to many of the Arsenal fans present at Wembley that day, Seaman appeared to be in tears of frustration at the end of the match.

There were times during the 1990–1 season when David Seaman seemed superhuman. The Cup semi-final proved otherwise.

But for those who suggested that he lacked the nerve for the big occasion, Seaman had something to say.

England's Number One gets some encouragement from Paul Gascoigne during the Euro 96 campaign

"There have been whispers that when it comes to big matches, David Seaman doesn't have the bottle. I take such suggestions as an insult. They disregard all the solid games I have been involved in, all the numerous matches where I have made crucial saves."

Interviewed by *The Sun*, David was typically honest in his appraisal of the semi-final: "On the day, the whole Arsenal side played well below the standards we had set in winning the Championship. The fact that we only conceded 18 goals in that campaign must have said something about me."

He was right. The semi-final was a personal nightmare, but over the course of the season, he had proved himself the best goalkeeper in Britain. The England manager Graham Taylor remained unconvinced, but Seaman was prepared to wait for another chance at international level. He also had plenty of support at Arsenal, notably from the club's goalkeeping coach, the former Gunners number one and Double winner, Bob Wilson.

The pair have forged a strong working relationship and a solid friendship during David's years at Highbury, and to the present day, Seaman still wears one of Wilson's old T-shirts in every game he plays for the Gunners. Wilson gave the shirt to Seaman as a good luck charm when the latter first arrived at the club. The shirt, plain white with a red BW on the chest, is getting a little tatty now. There are a few holes around the seams. But Seaman refuses to play without it. He even feels that the shirt is a part of him. And Bob keeps checking to make sure he's still wearing it for every game, too.

"Bob has helped me out a lot," David said. "He sees things like the keeper he was. Well," he joked, "you can't really take goalkeeping tips from your manager, can you?"

Every August, Seaman and Bob Wilson get together and set targets for the season ahead. David reckons that in an average season he will make six mistakes which lead directly to goals. Just like every other goalkeeper, David accepts that he cannot stop every shot, but this doesn't stop him striving for perfection.

David admits he is obsessively self-critical. If he makes an error in a game, he will watch a tape of the incident, freeze-framing the action time and time again until he has worked out exactly what went wrong and what can be done to prevent the same thing happening again. And then he'll run through his ideas with Bob Wilson, who will almost

"We don't always agree," says Seaman of coach Bob Wilson, "but he's helped me out a lot"

Working out with England

Long periods out of the action can only be overcome by staying totally focussed on the match

certainly have been analysing a tape of the match himself. "We don't always agree about things," David says, "but I need to be told if he thinks I can do things better."

David is also coached by England goalkeeping guru Mike Kelly, and believes that in Kelly and Wilson, he has the best advisers in the game. Their input is vital if David suffers a dip in confidence and a loss of form.

Despite the disaster in the cups, the 1990–1 season ended in triumph. Seaman picked up a cherished championship winners' medal, his first honour in 12 years of professional football.

Sadly, the following season was a disappointment for David and for Arsenal. They relinquished their league title to Liverpool and never really looked like the mean machine of '91. The Gunners were comprehensively outclassed by Benfica in the European Cup, then humbled by little Wrexham in the Third Round of the FA Cup in one of the most sensational upsets in Cup history.

The 1992–3 season also saw Arsenal failing to challenge for the championship, but in the cup competitions they were an irresistible force, thanks in no small part to the goalscoring of Ian Wright. And so it was that Arsenal and Spurs met once more in the semi-finals of the FA Cup in May 1993. Again the venue was Wembley, but this time there could be no mistakes and no excuses. Nothing but a win would suffice for the Arsenal fans, who could hardly believe the chance of revenge had come so soon.

The game was unbelievably tense. In extra time, Arsenal captain Tony Adams headed his side into the lead, but Spurs fought back, and with Lee Dixon sent off for a professional foul, the Gunners were hanging on desperately for the final ten minutes.

David Seaman was a giant in that game, and right at the death, with Arsenal fans screaming for the whistle, Seaman made a diving save at the feet of Teddy Sheringham which was as brave as it was brilliant and vital.

Not for the first time and not for the last, David Seaman was Arsenal's saviour.

The Gunners won the semi-final, avenging the painful defeat of '91, and went on to secure an unprecedented FA and Coca-Cola Cup double by beating Sheffield Wednesday in both finals.

Two more medals for ol' Safe Hands – but his greatest heroics were to come in the next three years, starting with Arsenal and a night of European drama which had to be seen to be believed...

Seaman in action in Euro 96 (*above*) a shot flies wide and (*opposite*) acknowledging the crowd

SEAMAN
1

England's Number One

The years 1994 to 1996 were exciting times for Arsenal and for England, and they saw David Seaman develop from pro's pro into an undisputed superstar.

Following their incredible domestic cup double, Arsenal entered the European Cup Winners' Cup in the 1993–4 season. The Gunners had failed miserably in the European Cup two years before, but this time the team was older and wiser and gave nothing away at the back, even when confronted with some of the most lethal strikers on the continent. Naturally, David Seaman was pivotal to Arsenal's success. In fact, the Gunners' defensive record in Europe was so good that a new anthem was taken up by the Arsenal fans. To the tune of 'Go West', the camp disco anthem recorded by the Village People and later by the Pet Shop Boys, the Gooners sang, 'One Nil To The Arsenal'. You don't sing that if you've got a dodgy 'keeper.

Fittingly, the Cup Winners' Cup final ended 1-0 to the Arsenal as Seaman and his trusty defenders shut out a Parma side spearheaded by an attacking trio of Gianfranco Zola, Faustino Asprilla and Thomas Brolin.

But if that was thrill-a-minute stuff, the next year's competition was even more heart-stopping. In the 1995 semi-final, Arsenal faced Italian giants Sampdoria. The first leg, at Highbury, finished 3–2 to the Gunners, setting up a night of intense drama in Genoa two weeks later.

Seaman's heroics in the Cup Winners' Cup semi-final were just part of an amazing three seasons for Arsenal and England

Sampdoria started the second leg sharply and were soon a goal up. Ian Wright pulled Arsenal level, but two goals in quick succession from the Italian sub Bellucci looked to have killed off the Cup holders. Not so. With two minutes on the clock, Stefan Schwarz scored with a free-kick and the game was tied on aggregate.

Extra time brought no more goals. It was time for the penalty shoot-out. Three years previously, David Seaman had saved three out of five penalties in the hostile atmosphere of The Den to beat Millwall in the Coca-Cola Cup, but against Sampdoria the big man was even better.

Seaman saved two of the Italians' first four penalties, but with Eddie McGoldrick and Paul Merson missing for Arsenal, the pressure was back on Seaman to stop Italian international Attillio Lombardo scoring with Sampdoria's fifth spot-kick. Lombardo struck it hard to the 'keeper's left, but incredibly, even as he dived low, Seaman managed to raise up a hand to claw the ball round the post.

Arsenal had done it. Seaman had done it. He was carried shoulder-high by his team-mates to the corner of the ground where the Arsenal fans celebrated wildly. Even now, that last save still looks impossible, but of course, David Seaman sees it a little differently to the rest of us, analysing the game as only a goalkeeper would.

"I had to do it in the penalty shoot-out," he told *The Daily Mail*, "because I let in three during normal time, which upset me."

David admitted he felt relieved that he was facing the penalties and not taking them. He wouldn't wish that kind of agony on anyone. The pressure, he reckons, is all on the taker. If the goalkeeper guesses right and dives the right way to make a save, he's a hero. If the penalty taker misses by an inch, he's a villain.

David doesn't like to say too much about his penalty-saving technique. It's a trade secret, after all. But he has revealed that he reads the penalty taker's run-up, judging how the player addresses the ball and then adjusting his own position accordingly. Clearly, that night in Genoa, his instinct and his reflexes were razor-sharp.

"With each save I made I felt better and better," he told pressmen after the game. "When I came off the field I just felt brilliant."

David's adrenaline levels were still sky high when the Arsenal team plane touched down in London, so when he got home at 4.30am, he watched the penalty shoot-out several times before retiring to bed. Thanks to David's heroics, team-mate Paul Merson was also able to sleep. Merson missed his penalty, but his keeper got him out of jail with that unbelievable third save. "David was outstanding," said an obviously relieved Merson. "He saved my skin."

David himself called that semi-final the best night of his career, but in football, fortunes can change from one game

Seaman established himself as England's best

to the next. It was David Seaman who got Arsenal to the 1995 Cup Winners' Cup final. And it was David Seaman who ended that final on his knees, tears in his eyes, wanting a huge hole to open up in the ground and swallow him up.

16,000 Arsenal supporters had made the short trip across the English Channel to the Parc de Princes in Paris for the final on May 10. Arsenal's opponents were Real Zaragoza of Spain, whose team included, of all people, a former Tottenham player, the Moroccan-born Nayim. Inevitably, Nayim became a prime target for the Arsenal boo-boys, but how he rammed the taunts back down the Gooners' throats. The match itself was nondescript. Zaragoza scored first through Esnaider. Then John Hartson, Arsenal's young

Seaman dives to save for England: the result of years of hard training paying off

Welsh striker, equalised. Once again, the Gunners faced extra time in a vital cup game, only this time it did not go to penalties. With just seconds remaining, and Arsenal fans already anticipating more miraculous penalty-saving from David Seaman, the ball fell to Nayim in the centre circle.

Seaman was positioned on the edge of his penalty area, poised to clear any long ball that was played into the Arsenal half. Nothing could have prepared him for what happened next.

Audaciously yet fortuitously, Nayim blasted a shot high into the night sky, over Seaman and into the net. Seaman made a desperate attempt to backtrack and get a hand to the ball. He got his fingers to it, but could only help the ball into the goal. Seaman came to rest in the net, the ball lying beside him. Nobody could quite believe it, not the Arsenal fans, nor the Zaragoza fans. They had just witnessed one of the most outrageous goals ever scored in European football. Zaragoza had won the Cup Winners' Cup, and David Seaman was desolate.

As the final whistle blew seconds after the restart, Seaman simply could not take in what had happened. Gazza's free-kick in 1991 was bad enough, he said, but this was worse. Much worse.

David maintains he was in the correct position. Goalkeepers often act as sweepers when a long ball is hit over a line of defenders playing offside. But as soon as Nayim hit the shot, Seaman knew he was in trouble.

If the semi-final had been the greatest night of the 'keeper's career, this was the worst. When the referee blew for full-time, Seaman slumped to the floor in utter despair.

"It hurt so much more than I have ever known," David told *The Daily Mail*. "But give him full credit because he meant it."

Nayim shrugged: "I saw Seaman off his line and then hit it over him. I don't know whether it was a brilliant goal or not. Maybe I just got lucky."

Stewart Houston was Arsenal's caretaker manager that night, having taken charge of first-team affairs mid-season following the sacking of George Graham over the bung scandal. Houston was quick to praise Seaman and remind the press that it was Seaman who had done more than any other player to get Arsenal to the final in the first place. Houston also pointed to several vital saves his goalkeeper had made during the 90 minutes of normal time, in particular a brilliant tip on to a post when a goal seemed certain.

Houston said it would be a pity if Seaman's performance against Sampdoria were to be forgotten because Nayim had beaten him from the halfway line. Football, Houston reminded us, is often a cruel game.

"It was a magnificent strike," he told *The Sun*, "the kind of thing you try 100 times and score just once."

As Seaman sat mutely in the dressing room, Houston stressed that no-one at Arsenal was blaming their 'keeper for the goal that cost them the Cup. How could Seaman be blamed after all he had done in the competition?

In the Arsenal dressing room, Bob Wilson was quick to console his old friend. Wilson knew the right things to say. He's been there himself during his long career.

And Tony Adams was soon doing his captain's job, telling the rest of the team to pick themselves up and get on the team coach, insisting that they would all be stronger for this experience. They would come back from it.

Watching McAllister's penalty fly off his elbow and away against Scotland in Euro 96

The mood on the flight home to London's Stansted airport was obviously subdued, but as Bob Wilson revealed, by the time the squad got off the plane at Stansted, David Seaman was grinning and laughing again. Life goes on, just as his dad had told him when he was rejected by Leeds all those years ago.

Of course there were people queuing up to take a shot at Seaman now. Four days after Paris, Arsenal visited Stamford Bridge for the final game of the Premiership season. As the Arsenal team emerged for the kick-in, the Chelsea fans began gleefully flapping their arms above their heads, chanting "Let's all do the Seaman" and "Nayim from the halfway line". Seaman smiled and waved back. The Chelsea fans applauded.

David admits there were times after that goal when he felt like staying indoors all day.

People would approach him in the street and then start running backwards, grasping at thin air, laughing their socks off. David can smile about it now, but at the time he wanted to chin them. It's not really his style, though, is it?

David Seaman is big enough to take the knocks. Given the setbacks that Seaman suffered, a lesser character might have given up on the dream of becoming England's number one 'keeper. But not Seaman. He always knew he was the best in the country. The problem was convincing former England boss Graham Taylor.

"I've had my fair share of bad moments with England," David recalls. "It took me a long time to feel as though I might be established as the number one."

David broke into the national squad when he was still at QPR and Bobby Robson was England manager. Robson gave him his first cap in a friendly in Saudi Arabia in 1991. Peter Shilton and Chris Woods were number one and number two back then, but David was confident that his time would come. He was still in his early 20s, and most great 'keepers don't reach their peak until they are past 30. To his delight, David was selected as the third keeper when Robson picked his squad for the 1990 World

Moment of triumph: Seaman celebrates the defeat of Spain in Euro 96

A study in patriotism as the National Anthem is played and Big Dave sings along

Cup Finals in Italy, but his joy soon turned to sadness when he broke a thumb in a freak accident in training. Seaman was sent home.

And worse was to come. Following Italia 90, Robson was replaced by Graham Taylor, who picked Seaman for a crunch European Championship qualifier against the Republic of Ireland and then blamed the 'keeper when England failed to win. Taylor claimed that Seaman was at fault for the Irish equaliser because he had not organised his defenders as efficiently as Peter Shilton would have done.

George Graham leapt to Seaman's defence, saying that Taylor's criticisms were both surprising and illogical. So what, said Graham, if Seaman did not shout orders at the England defenders like Shilton. "David doesn't talk a lot, but it never affects Arsenal's performance," Graham told *The Mirror*. "As far as I'm concerned David is still the best 'keeper in England."

Yet Graham Taylor was not alone in questioning Seaman's international calibre. After a friendly in Prague in 1992 against Czechoslovakia, *The Times* said that although Seaman's performances for Arsenal were consistently high, he could not be trusted at the highest level and was not the man for England.

"Seaman's ability is beyond dispute," *The Times* stated, "but his temperament was so evidently shaky against Czechoslovakia that Graham Taylor can scarcely afford to retain him even as understudy to Chris Woods."

And so David Seaman was discarded when England went to the 1992 European Championships in Sweden.

Balance, strength and timing in perfect harmony as Seaman kicks clear

Seaman arrives at Wimbledon with girlfriend Debbie, to a hero's welcome

"The first thing I knew about it was when I walked into a team meeting and was asked to leave the room," Seaman told *The Mail*. "That was the lowest point of my career. I didn't play for England again for 18 months."

Crystal Palace's Nigel Martyn was promoted to number two. England exited the tournament without a win.

Seaman returned for the qualifying stages of the 1994 World Cup, but was caught out by a canny free-kick from Dutch sweeper Ronald Koeman in the decisive group match in Rotterdam, and England were out.

As a footnote, Taylor and Seaman met in a Hertfordshire supermarket not long after Euro 96. Much to the amusement of other shoppers, Taylor dropped to his knees in mock homage to Seaman. The big fella laughed, of course.

Terry Venables, Taylor's successor, had no doubts about Seaman's ability or temperament. As far as Venables was concerned, the Arsenal man was England's automatic first choice 'keeper.

Seaman agreed. But he had set his sights even higher than England number one. David Seaman would love to be recognised as the best in goalkeeper in the world, and feels that his performances in Euro 96 can only have improved his worldwide standing.

England's first game of Euro 96 was a forgettable one for England and for Seaman. Pandemonium greeted Alan Shearer's opening strike against Switzerland, but Roy Hodgson's side were better organised than many had expected, and the Swiss ended up with a share of the points after Kubilay Turkyilmaz levelled from the penalty spot. David Seaman conceding a penalty? What happened?

"I've had my fair share of bad moments with England. It took me a long time to feel established"

"Maybe I put the odds in favour of Turkyilmaz by diving a shade too soon," David confessed. "I ended up going the wrong way."

Reaching for the top at Highbury

Seaman throws his arms wide in celebration as one goes in at the other end

England's second group match on June 15 saw England and Seaman transformed. The opposition were the auld enemy, Scotland. The game was billed as the Battle of Britain, and certainly, neither side dared contemplate defeat. Once again, it was Alan Shearer who opened the scoring, nodding in at the far post from Manchester United wing-back Gary Neville's teasing centre. But it took two incredible saves from David Seaman to keep England on course for victory.

With the score still at 1–0, Scotland won a penalty, but Seaman saved from Scottish skipper Gary McAllister, and within minutes, England scored again through Paul Gascoigne to settle the issue. However, Seaman reckons his other crucial save, this one from a Gordon Durie header, was even better than the penalty stop. As Durie headed towards the top left-hand corner of Seaman's goal, the keeper had to dive quickly to his left and palm the ball away. As every goalkeeper knows, such a save requires enormous strength in the wrist to get a firm contact on the ball at full stretch. This, says Seaman, is when a 'keeper finds out if he has what those in the profession call a 'chocolate wrist'. Needless to say, Seaman does not. He pushed Durie's effort around the post, then crashed into the upright himself.

Former England 'keeper Gordon Banks praised the save not merely for the agility and technique it necessitated, but also the bravery Seaman showed in risking injury to make sure he got to the ball. Without the saves from Durie and from McAllister, England might have drawn or even lost the Battle Of Britain. As it was, they ran out 2–0 winners, and then thumped the Dutch 4–1, with Seaman making another outstanding stop from his Arsenal clubmate and friend Dennis Bergkamp.

A brave save at the striker's feet whilst on international duty...

Then came Spain and arguably the greatest game of David Seaman's brilliant career that we recalled in chapter one. And next came Germany in the semi-final, and heartbreak for David, his England team-mates, and fans across the country. This time, Seaman could not save England in the penalty shoot-out. The Germans simply didn't give him a chance of saving even one spot-kick. And poor Gareth Southgate missed his.

"I am not usually the most emotional of people," Seaman told *The Mail*, "but tears welled up in my eyes – as they did in Stuart Pearce's, Gazza's and of course Gareth's."

After the defeat, the England players returned to the team hotel in Burnham Beeches to reflect on what might have been. Darren Anderton and Gazza had come so close to winning the game for England in extra time. For an hour, everybody sat around staring at the walls and saying little, but eventually the mood lightened as the players shared a few jokes and a few beers.

Each player went individually to console Southgate, and eventually even he smiled again.

These players had lost a game, but they had made everyone in the country feel proud to be English.

"We came so close to fulfilling everyone's dreams," David Seaman sighs. "Euro 96 was a wonderful occasion for the whole country."

And an occasion which turned the big goalkeeper and quiet, friendly man into a full-blown national hero!

Gentle Giant

"In a crowd of people, I'll just keep quiet and hope that no-one notices me," says David Seaman, adding with a smile, "it's pretty hard when you're 6ft 4in."

David Seaman has always stuck out from the crowd. Even when he was at school, he was taller than most kids' dads, and was always picked to go in goal because he was so big. Now, of course, David is a truly imposing figure. Most footballers are bigger in the flesh than they appear on the pitch or on a TV screen. One Arsenal fan once remarked that even Glenn Helder, the slender and skilful Dutch winger, is built like a brick outhouse. David Seaman is built like a very big brick outhouse, weighing in at over 15 stones, all of it muscle. As The *Sunday Times* once described David: "He is huge every way you look at him, upwards, backwards, sideways. His hands, like paddles, rest on oak trunk thighs."

Small wonder, then, that everyone from George Graham to Bob Wilson to new Arsenal manager Arsene Wenger describe David Seaman as a goalkeeping giant with a genuinely commanding presence. It has been said that when Seaman enters a room, he fills it. This was certainly true of the time Seaman popped into the players' lounge at Ewood Park after Arsenal played Blackburn Rovers in 1996. Seaman simply dwarfed the likes of Alan Shearer and

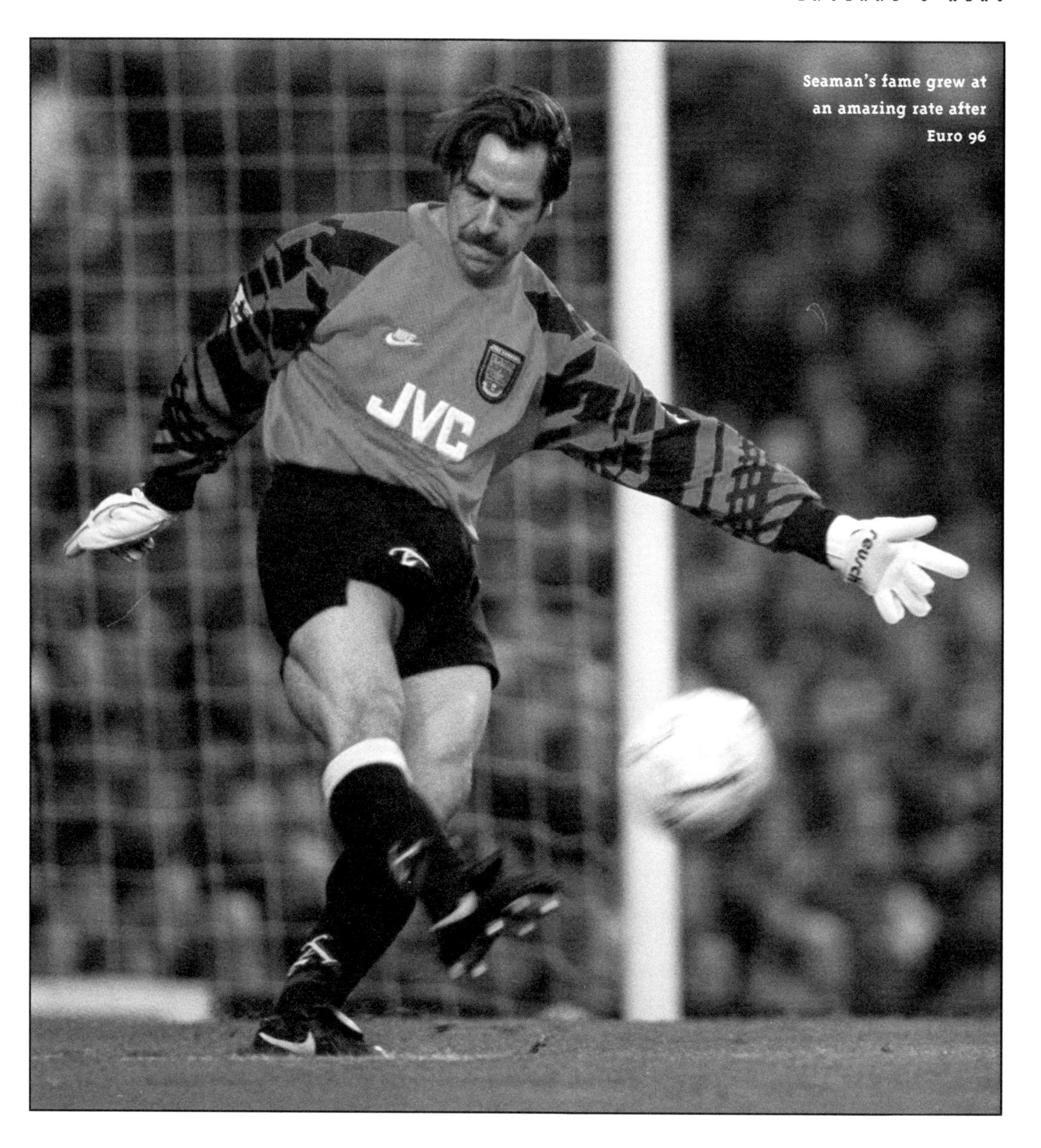

Seaman's fame grew at an amazing rate after Euro 96

David Platt. Autograph hunters had no trouble finding the big 'keeper, and they all got a friendly welcome.

David's remarkable career is well documented, but what is the big Yorkshireman like off the pitch? What does 'Safe Hands' Seaman do when he's not saving England and Arsenal's bacon and making himself the hero in penalty shoot-outs and important cup finals? How does he keep his composure under the pressures of big-time football?

"He's got oak-trunk thighs..."

Colleague and friend Bob Wilson says of David: "He is one of the most human people I know."

Compared to most footballers, there's very little that's flash about David Seaman. Maybe it's something he learnt from his upbringing in Yorskhire.

After his brilliant performances in Euro 96, every newspaper in Britain wanted a sensational new story about England's number one. What the papers found was a relaxed, easy-going bloke, one of football's most popular characters, who works hard at his game and enjoys a good laugh now and then. David was even able to laugh off the attentions of the press pack.

In action against Spurs in the 1991 Cup semi-final: David's calm nature enabled him to come back

"It's really stressful at times," he confessed, "a real invasion, but all you can do is laugh about it afterwards."

The story that most interested the papers concerned David's divorce and his subsequent romance with former Arsenal employee Debbie Rodgers.

"He's not like some footballers," Debbie told *The Daily Mirror*. "Not in the least bit laddish."

The couple's relationship grew and survived a tabloid inquisition.

Whenever David has played at Highbury, Debbie has been there to cheer him on. And surprisingly, she says she's rarely nervous when she watches him play.

Looking back at the break-up of his marriage, David reflects: "It was pretty rough, but it didn't affect me as a player. You've got to put your problems to the back of your mind. It's part of being a footballer." This attitude to life's ups and downs is typical of David Seaman. If you've got problems, he says, you just have to get on with life and work things out.

David says he learnt at an early age that you have to try to be happy in your life. Problems will always come along. It's how you deal with them that matters, and how quickly you put those problems behind you. David applies the same logic to his goalkeeping. Confidence comes from within. That's why David Seaman keeps telling himself he's the best.

Now David is looking forward to a future with Debbie and Debbie feels that she and David have been through so much together, it is like they have been together for ten years, not three.

"We do everything together," Debbie says, "apart from his golfing and fishing. We're a homely pair."

"I don't really go out with the lads," says David. "If I go out, it's with Debbie to a restaurant."

True to his word, when David was out in Hong Kong several years ago with the England team, and most of the players went out on a booze bender which led to the infamous 'dentist's chair' incident, David got an early night. So when Gazza and the rest of the lads were strapped into the so-called 'dentist's chair', having potent cocktails poured down their throats, David Seaman was fast asleep and dreaming about saving penalties.

Off the field, David relaxes with overnight fishing trips: Even those help his concentration in goal

That's why George Graham called Seaman the perfect pro, although David has since revealed that he was gutted when he found out what happened on that night in Hong Kong. Seaman said it sounded like a great night.

However, when he's back at home in Hertfordshire, where he lives with Debbie in a mansion in Chorleywood which was once owned by actor James Mason, David is happier just relaxing rather than going out on the town with the Arsenal lads.

He even helps with the shopping, and says he's not ashamed to do the ironing or run the Hoover around the house!

And it was with Debbie that David attended Buckingham Palace on a bright day in early 1997, when the Queen awarded him the MBE for 'services to association football'. On the steps of the Palace, David beamed: "I am a very proud man. The biggest problem has being not being able to tell anyone. Debbie and I have been bursting to tell the world. It's such a great end to a great year, the best of my life."

Away from football, David enjoys various sports including golf and swimming. A natural athlete, he can strike a golf ball fully 300 yards, and is renowned on the tennis courts for his thunderous serve.

Bob Wilson also remarks that David can swim like Johnny Weissmuller, the former Olympic swimming champ who went on to star in the movies as Tarzan!

However, when he really wants to get away from it all, when he needs a little time to himself, to be alone with his thoughts, David Seaman goes fishing. He reckons that fishing helps his football too, because it develops his powers of concentration and teaches him to be patient, both vital qualities for a top class goalkeeper who might be inactive for huge periods of a game but will need his reflexes to be sharp whenever he is called into action by the opposition.

David loves to go fishing all night at a lake close to his house. He will leave the house at five in the afternoon armed with a rod and tackle and a sleeping bag. He sets up line and settles down for a kip, with the line rigged so that

Seaman's size is a big asset

David has got a lot more to achieve in football before he hangs up those big ol' gloves!

it triggers an alarm to wake him up if a fish bites. Night is the best time to catch carp, which David regards as one of the most difficult fish to catch. He recently caught his best-ever fish, a 20lb monster carp on an all-night, all-action trip.

On a still night, fishing by a lake, David Seaman finds total peace of mind. Sometimes, David even has his England team-mate Paul Gascoigne for company. Gazza loves the peace and quiet of fishing too. David reckons he sees a side of Gazza that few people get to see, a quieter and more reflective side to the wayward genius. But while Gazza understands David's angling obsession, the rest of the Arsenal squad do not. They're constantly ribbing the keeper about staying out all night in the cold and rain just to hook one measly fish, but as David points out, he can stand out in the cold and rain all night at Highbury sometimes and he'll only have one catch to make.

David dreams of running his own fishery when he retires from football, but that, of course, is a long time off. The big fella has got much more to achieve in football before Arsenal and England allow him to hang up those big old gloves and head for the riverbank on a permanent basis!

Back To The Future

With over 200 appearances for Arsenal and over 30 full England caps to his name, David Seaman MBE is firmly established as one of the finest British footballers of all time. With Arsenal he has won all three major domestic honours; a league championship medal (1991), an FA Cup winners' medal (1993) and a League Cup winners' medal (1993). To this he can add a European Cup Winners' Cup winners' medal (1994) and a runners-up medal from the following year (1995).

But still Seaman is hungry for more. He has his heart set on winning even more trophies with the Gunners, and on winning something with England. With footballers' careers growing ever longer thanks to careful dieting and expert physiotherapy, and with goalkeepers capable of staying at the very top of the game until well into their forties, who would bet against Seaman collecting more and more honours?

"It's everyone's ambition to play in the World Cup," David told *The Daily Mail* following his and England's heroics in Euro 96. "We all got a taste of how good big tournaments can be during Euro 96, and obviously I'd love to play in the World Cup. But," he adds warily, "I don't tempt fate, because football has a habit of kicking you in the teeth."

If David Seaman ever needed reminding of just how quickly things can go wrong in this game, he need only cast his mind back to that Nayim goal, or Gazza's and

Working hard on the training ground to make sure his career stays in top shape...

Koeman's free-kicks, or the day that a 19-year-old Yorkshire lad was told he wasn't good enough to play for the team he had loved ever since he was big enough to kick a football. But as David's Arsenal and England team-mate Tony Adams always says when the going gets really tough, what doesn't kill you makes you stronger. David Seaman is as strong as they come.

So what does the future hold for Seaman? One thing is for certain: he won't be shaving off his moustache ever again.

"I tried it once," he says. The young 'keeper went clean-shaven for a Leeds United team photograph in 1981. It didn't look right, David says. And seeing as he was kicked out of the club mere months later, shaving the 'tache was hardly a good omen.

But on a more serious note, what lies ahead for the big man? At club level, there appear to be exciting times ahead for Seaman in Arsene Wenger's Arsenal revolution.

All the players at the club have said how refreshing Wenger's new regime has proven. New training methods and new tactics have revitalised the club. The "boring, boring" Arsenal of old has been transformed into a potent attacking force, but of course, any team who intend to challenge for major honours needs a solid defence. As such, the value and influence of David Seaman cannot be understated. All of Seaman's team-mates say the same thing, that the man radiates confidence which flows through the whole team. In the heat of a crunch Premiership match at Old Trafford or Anfield, or in a hazardous FA Cup tie in a small Second Division ground, you need a cool head and a sure pair of hands between the sticks. David Seaman is cool personified. His hands are the safest in the business. No wonder Arsenal have given Seaman a lengthy new contract. They would be mad to let him go.

After his amazing saves in the Cup Winners' Cup penalty shoot-out against Sampdoria, there were rumours in the British press that a big Italian club was about to launch a £5m raid for Seaman. There was uncertainty at Arsenal because manager George Graham had only recently been sacked. Arsenal fans panicked. Selling Seaman would be nothing short of suicidal. Everyone around Highbury breathed a sigh of relief when Seaman signed another contract with the club. David Seaman is as vital to Arsenal

Selling Seaman would have been 'nothing short of suicidal' for Arsenal. And the fans would have had their say, too!

Football Club as captain Tony Adams. And the same applies to England. Seaman may have begun his international career tentatively, he may have suffered harsh criticism in the British press from football writers and even from the England manager himself, but he now stands proud as England's undisputed number one. Throughout the country there are many excellent goalkeepers, men like Nigel Martyn at Leeds United, Tim Flowers at Blackburn Rovers and Ian Walker at Tottenham Hotspur. But they will have to wait for their chance, just as David Seaman did when Peter Shilton and then Chris Woods made the England 'keeper's jersey their own. David Seaman is the number one now, and he plans on sticking around for many years to come. Not only that, but he still yearns to be acknowledged as the number one 'keeper in the world.

When David Seaman talks about Gordon Banks, the goalkeeper in England's 1966 World Cup winning side, and the fact that people all over the country still talk about the save that Banks made from the great Pele in the 1970 World Cup Finals, it is clear that Seaman himself strives for the same legendary status as Banks.

After Euro 96, when Seaman's brilliance outshone his great rival in the Premiership, Manchester United's Danish international Peter Schmeichel, Seaman told *The Daily Mail*: "I hope the saves I have made have enhanced my claim to be world number one. That is what I want. To be the best in

David takes a well-earned break during an England training session

Bob Wilson has played a major role in Seaman's success

SIMPLY THE BEST: OTHER STARS ON SEAMAN

Gordon Banks (former England goalkeeper)
"David Seaman was not only England's Euro 96 saviour, but the finest goalkeeper in the tournament, which makes him one of the best in the world. I admire his all-round game, the way he comes for crosses and dominates the box and the way he punches the ball only when necessary. It must give his defenders great confidence knowing that he is the last line of defence."

Stewart Houston (former Arsenal caretaker-manager)
"What can you say about a guy like David? He is the number one, no doubt about that."

Bob Wilson (Arsenal goalkeeping coach)
"David Seaman will make mistakes for the rest of his career; so will Peter Schmeichel, and they are the two top goalkeepers in the country by a mile. As a goalkeeper, the thing you are judged on is how many mistakes you make And I think David makes fewer in a season than Peter."

Terry Venables (former England coach)
"As far as I am concerned David Seaman is automatic first choice for England."

Anders Limpar (former Arsenal team-mate)
"When players come through alone on him, he is a wall."

Arsenal's number one – for a few more years yet...

David Seaman: All-round nice guy and probably the best goalkeeper in the world

the world, you have to be involved in a successful side in a major tournament."

With Glenn Hoddle's England growing stronger with each game, Seaman's dream can become a reality. Thanks to Seaman's inspirational goalkeeping, England came heart-breakingly close to glory in Euro 96. Perhaps victory will finally come in one of the next big tournaments. If it happens, no Englishman will be prouder than David Seaman.

"It's my ambition to do what only one goalkeeper has done before," Seaman told *FourFourTwo* magazine. "Win something with England. That and win the Premier League, because it's such a big trophy and I'd love to get my hands on that." He has a wonderful chance this season with Arsene Wenger's revitalised team.

David Seaman has big dreams, but then he always has done, ever since he was a schoolboy dreaming of becoming England goalkeeper. If the schoolboy's dream came true, why not the others?

David Seaman has earned his success. Since childhood, he has worked hard at improving his game. As a kid, he would carry an orange or a tennis ball with him at all times, so he could keep squeezing and squeezing the object in order to build up his hand and wrist strength. It sounds stupid, but it paid off when Seaman pushed that penalty round the post against Spain and the whole country rose to salute England's number one.

That's David Seaman: salt-of-the-earth Yorkshire lad, and probably the best goalkeeper in the world.

Big Dave smiles at another terrible joke in England training

David Seaman:
England's hero!